When I grow up,
I want to...

Help People

NoodleJUICE

Noodle Juice Ltd
www.noodle-juice.com
Stonesfield House, Stanwell Lane, Great Bourton, Oxfordshire, OX17 1QS
First published in Great Britain 2023
Copyright © Noodle Juice Ltd 2023
Text by Noodle Juice 2022
Illustrations by Flavio Remontti 2022
All rights reserved
Printed in China
A CIP catalogue record of this book is available from the British Library.
ISBN: 978-1-915613-05-9
1 3 5 7 9 10 8 6 4 2

This book is made from FSC®-certified paper. By choosing this book, you help to take care of the world's forests. Learn more: www.fsc.org

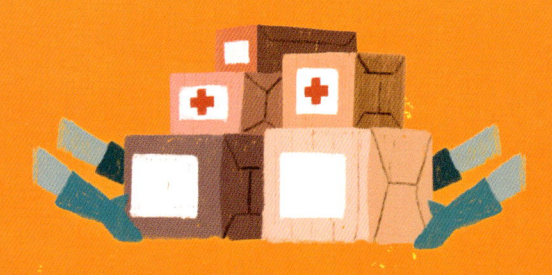

Contents

4 Teacher
6 Charity Worker
8 Fitness Instructor
10 Police Officer
12 Translator
14 Nutritionist
16 Paramedic
18 Sports Coach
20 Career Advisor
22 Doctor
24 Care Worker
26 Yoga Teacher
28 Nurse
30 People Who Help

This is a teacher.

Teachers help us to learn to **read and write**. They help us learn how to add up.

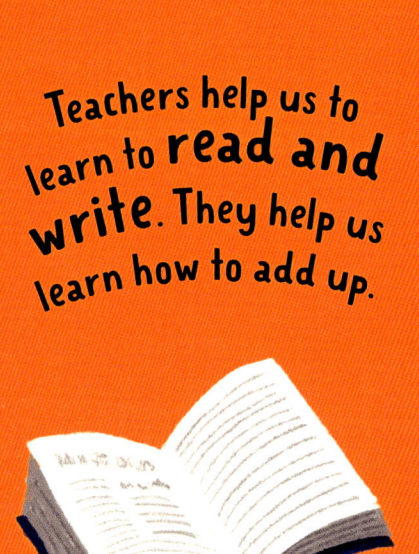

Teachers also help us to **understand** other people's cultures and what it's like to live in other parts of our world.

Bonjour!

OLÁ!

HELLO!

¡Hola!

Teachers can speak to us in other **languages** and help us learn to do the same.

Teachers show us how to **respect** each other and our planet.

Happy

Sad

They help us to express our **feelings** through words or pictures.

Teachers are very important because they are training the **next generation** to think better.

Future
Technology
Health
Wellbeing

Teachers also make sure we know how to play games and be good **team players**.

Teachers help people.

This is a charity worker.

Charity workers help people who are **struggling** with life.

Some charity workers help people who have suffered from **natural disasters**, such as floods or hurricanes.

NO WORK
NO VACANCIES
NO FOOD

Some charity workers help people who have had to leave their homes due to **fighting** or hunger.

Other charity workers support people who don't have any money for **food**, or who are ill.

They help by **fundraising**. They persuade people to donate money, have a charity cake sale or go on a sponsored run.

Charity workers also persuade governments and businesses to **contribute** as well.

Some charity workers travel to other countries, where they help to organise food and **medical supplies**.

Charity workers help people.

This is a fitness instructor.

Fitness instructors help us to **exercise**.

KEEP YOUR BACK STRAIGHT.

ADJUST YOUR LEGS!

Exercise helps to keep us **fit and healthy**. It makes us feel better about ourselves.

GOOD!

GREAT!

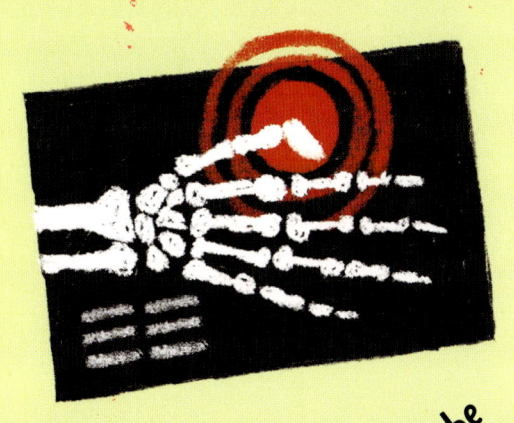

Fitness instructors need to be aware of any **illness** or **injury** someone might have.

They create **different programmes** to suit each person's needs.

LIGHT
REGULAR
HARD

Fitness instructors can hold **classes** for lots of people to enjoy.

DOING GREAT!

KEEP GOING!

They encourage people to **keep going** even when exercise feels like hard work.

Fitness instructors help people.

This is a police officer.

Police officers help to keep people **safe**.

I FEEL SAFE.

They work in local communities to **protect people** and prevent crime.

Some police officers investigate crimes such as **theft** or vandalism. Others look for missing people.

Some police officers make sure our **roads** are safe for drivers and pedestrians.

Police officers sometimes need to **testify in court** so that criminals go to prison.

I SWEAR!

In an emergency, police officers help to keep everyone **calm** and make sure they know what needs to happen next.

Police officers help people.

This is a translator.

Translators and interpreters help us to understand **different languages**.

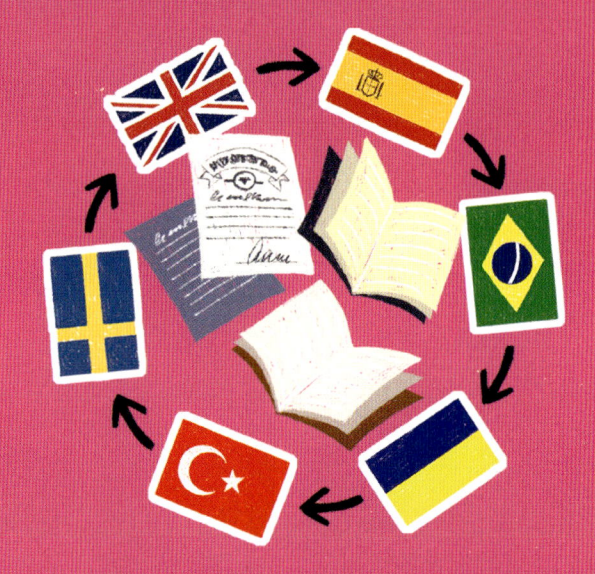

Translators change **books and documents** from one language to another.

HITOTSU NO SEKAI

ONE WORLD

EEN WERELD

They have to be **accurate** to make sure that people understand exactly what the words say.

Interpreters change one **spoken or sign** language into another.

COMMENT VOUS SENTEZ-VOUS?

HOW DO YOU FEEL?

I FEEL WELL

Interpreters can help doctors in a hospital communicate with their patients if they don't **share a language**.

Some interpreters help in dangerous situations, such as war or famine. Others work with **refugees**.

Translators and interpreters help people.

This is a nutritionist.

Nutritionists help people who need **advice and support** on their diet.

It is important to **educate people** about the benefits of eating well.

Some nutritionists work with **individuals** to develop specific food programmes that make them feel better.

Sports nutritionists work with teams or athletes to develop a diet that gives them the **energy** they need.

Some nutritionists work with **animals** instead of people.

Other nutritionists work with businesses or **research institutes** to make sure the food we eat is healthy.

Nutritionists help people.

This is a paramedic.

Paramedics are often the first people to help us if we have been in an **accident** or are suddenly unwell.

HELP! HELP!

They are sometimes called '**first responders**'.

Paramedics transport patients in **ambulances** and sometimes in helicopters.

It is their job to make **quick decisions** about their patients' treatment before moving them.

NOW!

YOU'LL BE FINE.

They work hard in **stressful** circumstances to help injured people.

Paramedics are caring and helpful people who try to make their patients **feel better**.

HELP!

Paramedics help people.

This is a sports coach.

Sports coaches or PE teachers help **athletes** of all ages and abilities to improve their performance.

Some coaches support a team as volunteers. Some make a career out of helping others to **do their best**.

18

They make sure that we are **fit and healthy** and know how our bodies work.

They understand the **rules and skills** needed for lots of different sports.

Sports coaches make sure we know how to work and play **together** well.

Sports coaches **inspire** the athletes they work with.

Sports coaches help people.

This is a career advisor.

A career advisor helps people to work out what they **want to do** as a job or a career.

MY CAREER

PLAN A   PLAN B   PLAN C

GREAT FUTURE!

They look at what you know, **what you're good at** and what you want to do to give you choices.

Career advisors need to know about many **different** jobs.

They help people to make the best out of their **education and skills**.

Career advisors often provide a **new way** of looking at things.

They can work in **schools** and local communities, as well as colleges and universities.

Career advisors help people.

21

This is a doctor.

Doctors help us when we are sick or have been hurt. They make us **well** again.

Doctors promise to **do no harm** in their medical career.

Some doctors work in the local community. Other doctors work in **hospitals** and clinics.

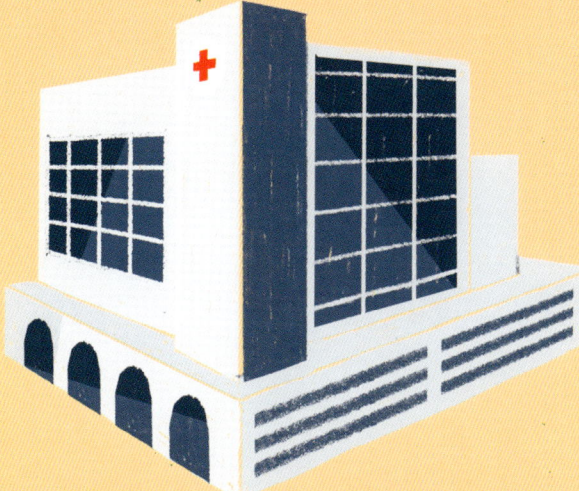

Some doctors choose to study parts of the **body or diseases**, such as the brain or cancer.

Other doctors choose to work in countries where people are suffering from **war or hunger**.

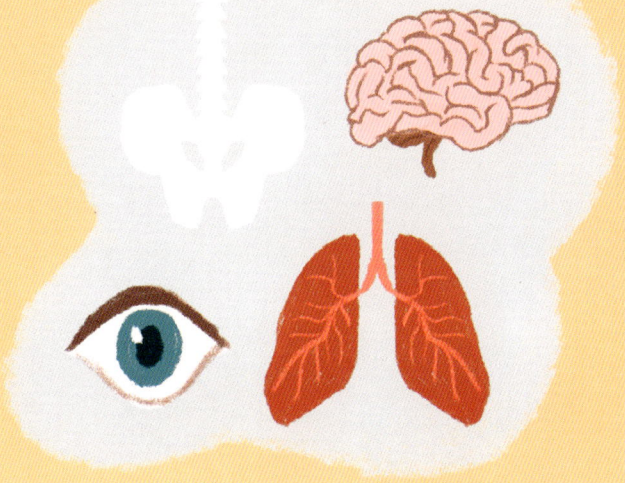

Doctors work with lots of other people to help **take care of us**.

Doctors help people.

23

This is a care worker.

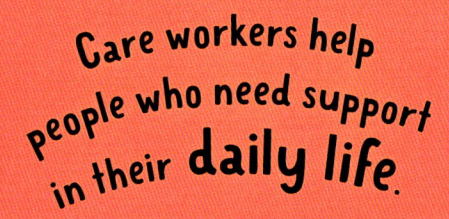

Care workers help people who need support in their **daily life**.

This can often be as simple as **preparing a meal**, going shopping or cleaning.

I'VE GOT YOUR BACK!

They may help someone attend a **doctor's appointment** or drive them to a hairdresser.

I'M HERE FOR YOU.

Care workers work with **children**, elderly people or people with disabilities.

Care workers like working with people and enjoy helping them to **feel better** about life.

HI, MR LOPEZ!

They can work in a person's home or in larger communities. Sometimes they are the **only person** someone might see.

Care workers help people.

25

This is a yoga teacher.

Yoga teachers help us to learn how to do **yoga poses**.

There are many different positions, with names such as '**downward facing dog**' or '**peaceful warrior**'.

Yoga teachers also help us to **meditate** and breathe properly.

INHALE

EXHALE

Yoga helps to keep our bodies healthy and **supple**.

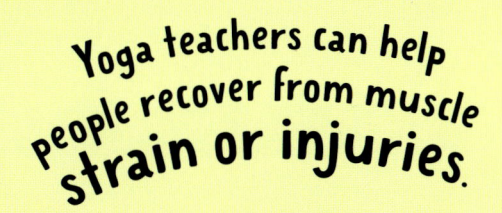

Yoga teachers can help people recover from muscle **strain or injuries**.

PRESS THIS MUSCLE.

Yoga is also relaxing and can help us to be **mindful**.

Yoga teachers help people.

27

This is a nurse.

Nurses help doctors to look after people who are ill or have been hurt.

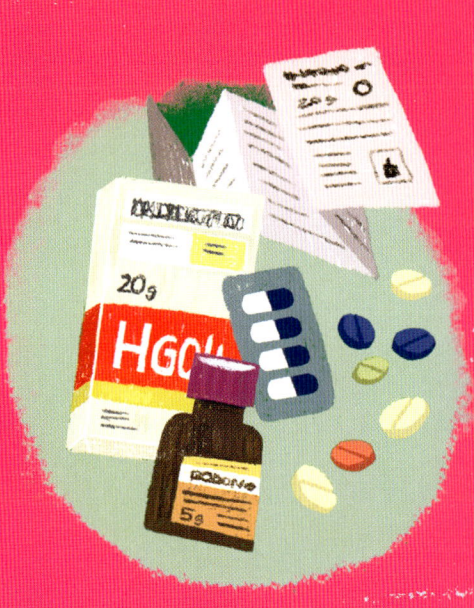

HE'S STABLE.

They care for patients by making sure they have the **medicine** or treatment that their doctor has chosen.

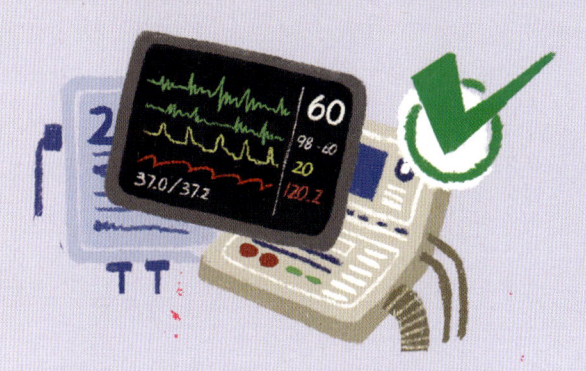

Some nurses work in **hospitals** on wards. Other nurses work in a doctor's surgery or the community.

Nurses have to check to see how their patients are **feeling** and keep the doctors up to date.

STAYING HEALTHY

Some nurses visit **schools** to teach children about staying healthy.

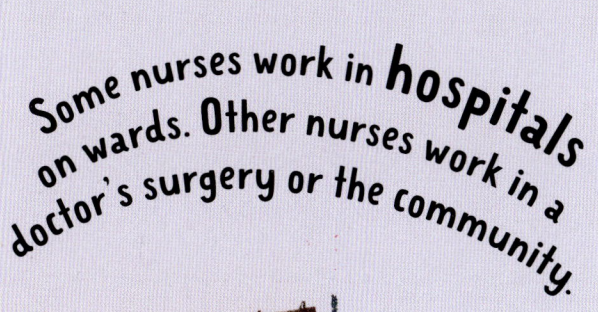

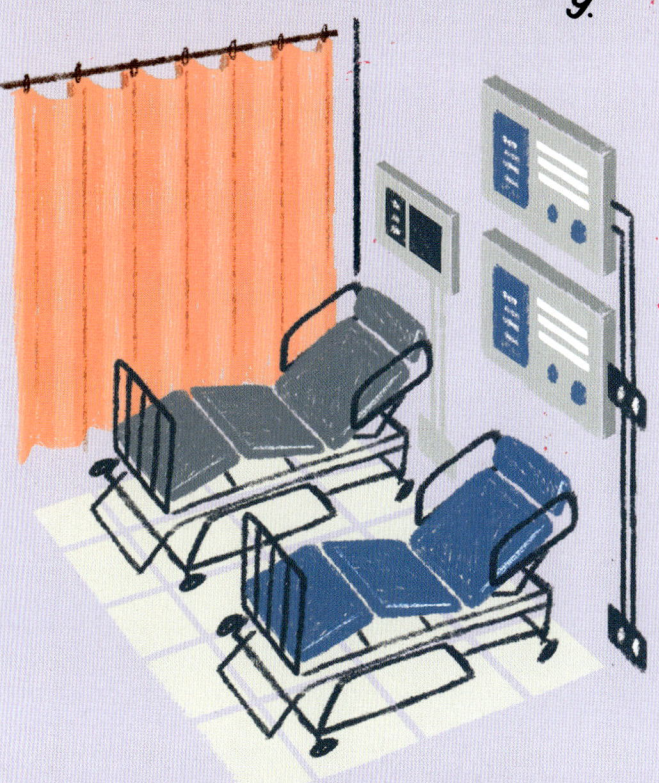

Some nurses help by working in **other countries**, where there might not be many doctors.

Nurses help people.

29

There are so many different ways to help people.

Nutritionist

Yoga teacher

Charity worker

Fitness instructor

Teacher

Police officer

Doctor

Translator

Care worker

Sports coach

Career advisor

Paramedic

Nurse

Which one will you choose?